THE FLOW LIFE FUNNEL

*The Eight Layers to Outwardly Live
What You Inwardly Desire*

Eva Payne

And That Which is Creativity

Disclaimer:

The purpose of this material is to educate and entertain. The author or publisher does not guarantee anyone following the techniques, suggestions, ideas, tips, or strategies will become successful. The author and publisher shall have neither liability nor responsibility to anyone with respect to any loss or damage caused, or alleged to be caused, directly or indirectly by the information contained in this book.

Dedicated

To my children, Emmi, Coleman, Brayden, Evan, Avery, and Dawson. You are each beautiful, whole, unique, and talented. May you always be in your own flow. I love you with all my everything.

To You, the seeker of more clarity. May the words in this book resonate with the parts of you that need to hear it most.

Acknowledgement

I am so grateful for my family, friends, and supporters who have validated my ideas are not crazy. Thank you Kristen, my Sis, for always believing in me and allowing me the opportunity to use your life as a test subject for this material. I am super grateful to my best friend and podcast co-host, Shelley Garite who would listen to all my ideas around flow, contribute her feedback, and hold space for me along this journey as I struggled with self-doubt. I am blessed to have a partner, Julian Archuleta who is patient, kind, and loving as I spent hours on this endeavor talking his ear off and never once giving me a hard time for being immersed in this work. Thank you to Mila the cover designer, and Kaitlyn Keller for editing. To Sky Nelson-Isaacs and Sarah Gregg, my friends, fellow Flow authors and Mastermind group partners, without your support, this manuscript would still be sitting on my computer. Jake Kelfer, your business coaching advice to take a bunch of jumbled up ideas and write it out on a whiteboard, made this book possible. I am grateful for all the beta readers, and all the publishing rejection letters. I learned something beautiful with each interaction. Finally, thank you for taking the time to explore how the Flow Life Funnel can improve your quality of life.

To purchase the book in bulk at a discount for your school, team, or organization or to sign up for Eva's email list at visit: ***www.evapayne.com***
Eva's podcast, SET 2 LOVE (Flow for Life) can be found at **www.set2love.com**

Table of Contents

Dedicated _____ iii

Acknowledgement _____ iv

Table of Contents _____ vi

PREFACE _____ viii

INTRODUCTION_____ 1

THE EIGHT PRINCIPLES OF THE FLOW LIFE
FUNNEL _____ 14

Principle One: INTUITION_____ 15
   Activities: Raise Your Intuition Activities _____ 21

Principle Two: INTERESTS _____ 25
   Discover Your Interests_____ 31

Principle Three: STRENGTHS (fixed) & Principle
Four: TALENTS/SKILLS (growth):_____ 32
   Activities: Discover the You that is Really You ___ 40

Principle Five: PASSION _____ 42
   Activities: Cultivate Passion _____ 49

Principle Six: BELIEF _____ 50
   Activities: Build Belief _____ 55

Principle Seven: NEED _____ **56**

Activities: Needs are Meant to be Filled _____ 62

Principle Eight: POOL OF CREATIVITY _____ **64**

Activities: Swim in the Pool of Creativity_____ 73

EXAMPLE OF THE FLOW LIFE FUNNEL IN USE 75

POURING THE PIECES INTO THE FUNNEL_____ 79

FINAL THOUGHTS _____ **81**

ABOUT THE AUTHOR _____ **86**

PREFACE

I have this innate ability to sit down with somebody, have a conversation, and at the end, suggest 10 possible solutions to their current challenges in life. When I begin my conversations, I quickly slip into a flow state and my mind starts racing through ideas faster than I can articulate. I have no idea what will work and what will not. What I do know is the more open and self-aware they are, the easier it is for me to act as an idea generating tool that helps them to sift through all the possibilities. This interaction allows the person I am talking with to see new strategies they never thought of, which may be worth trying.

One cool winter morning, I sat next to a gentleman on a flight home from Oakland to Burbank, and in the course of the trip, I THINK I helped him come up with a new job / plan for life. I don't usually talk to the people next to me on planes, but he looked rather nervous. When I asked him if he was okay, he said he flies all the time, but going home gets him so excited. He traveled a lot for his job, which kept him from being with his fiance. He had a very niche job selling super expensive, high end cars to multimillionaires. He could tell you anything and everything about the cars they only make a handful of, ever. My objective was to figure out how to keep him home more.

Over the course of the trip, we were able to kindle ideas that may lead to other ideas for him down the road. I simply helped his mind shift out from the patterns he was used to thinking. He was so excited that he introduced me to his fiance and said, "Eva may have just changed our lives." This got me wondering, how do I do this and can it be explained or taught? This is when I feel the most in FLOW, when I am coming up with ideas that will help solve a problem or fill a need. I can see connections and shuffle through the noise.

Our world is hurting, and in more ways than any of us can really comprehend. We are suffering on individual levels and we are suffering collectively, as a community on Earth, and it's my estimation that we are probably suffering on an even larger scale that simply hasn't yet been recognized or discovered. But, there is so much hope. For there is always something meaningful to hold onto, even in the darkest of times.

So, yes, there are horrible, sad, and heartbreaking events in our world everyday, but there is also so much good out there! Where we put our focus is what will grow. And my goal, along with so many others, is to help us all become part of the solution to our small and large challenges. All the answers we ever need for our life is right within reach, either internally or externally. We just need to take the next step, not the next hundred. Lay just one brick a day.

We have the people in our lives already who can lead us to more of the "right people" so that we can reach a new level of self-leadership and fulfillment. This will transpire if we can open our minds and hearts to see it and have the courage to leap into the unknown. We have access to the internet and experts in all areas at our fingertips. We have the ability to research solutions to challenges and connect with others who are also researching possible solutions. The answers are logical, but may take a creative and innovative approach. The answers will come when we can be self aware, and then willing to share our essence with others who have a similar vision and passion.

Whenever I dive into someone's life story, while at a wedding or standing in line at Disneyland or Walmart, I can see the pain. I empathize to the best of my ability, then I can see the good through all that sadness, confusion, or challenges. I can see numerous paths this individual could take to possibly a more joyful place. Will all the possible ideas work? I have no clue and that part isn't my work, but theirs. It is not my job as a Mother, a Friend, a Sister, and Partner to push anyone to BE anything. The choice, to be in FLOW, has to come from them, through following their own intuition and their own heart.

The world is hurting. But, we have the answers! We have all the answers to all the biggest problems. We just need to have the courage to go after the solutions using everything that makes us, us. It's really that simple. For example, let's say you are super, uber passionate about infertility; you could use your superpowers to make a difference in this need. One person might chase a cure. One person might chase the history and subsequent cause. One person might create supportive spaces for those looking for resources. One person might offer solutions to what can be done right now to heal from the pain or find hope. One person will have a need, and another will fill it. Both are winners. Both grow in love and human connection. Both are grateful. This is FLOW synergy.

This is a possible step to healing the world. Imagine if you used your essence to fit into the larger picture of life's evolution. What if you knew what you had to add, and could do it with more ease, fun, and meaning? When we are confident in what we have to offer, we seem to do it more openly. Within this openness comes the space for creative collaborations. Within these kinds of collaborations, where the pursuit of devotion and love is shared, magic happens and life flows.

When we truly collaborate, authentically, wholeheartedly putting in our time, talents, and treasures, toward experiences which could lead to more joy, we flow. We will change the game of life forever when we are living in alignment with our authentic essence. We can show up for ourselves and for another, with an open intention to serve, doing the best we can. If you feel as though you are spending a majority of your day and life in an unfulfilled way, this funnel will assist you to tip into 51% joy. Life can be about pushing toward a goal, keeping the ego filled, or the bank account. Life can also be about filling your half empty or half full cup with love and a spark for life as it is right now. This offers the freedom to follow life's opportunities wholeheartedly by living open and finding value in everything.

I desire for the world to be a more harmonious place tomorrow than it is today. That starts with one person making a small choice to lay one brick toward their true FLOW life. Progress is progress, and I can't wait for it to unfold at whatever pace it needs to unfold for you. We can learn patience and efficiency through the learning journey of how best to execute our dreams within this given human experience. There is a dream inside of you and it is asking you to take small or large steps toward the future you want to create for yourself, and your circle of influence. Joy is experienced in the journey of pursuing devotion, passion, love. Fall in love with the process of life, and you can find joy in each day.

> *"Love, like a river, will cut a new path whenever it meets an obstacle."*
>
> – Crystal Middlemas

INTRODUCTION

What if you made a wholehearted commitment to yourself right now, that no matter what you read, or hear about The Flow Life Funnel, you will be in the deepest pursuit of what brings your heart the greatest joy? How would your life change if you REALLY went after one of your life purposes? I believe that when we are in pursuit of our personal greatness, we live in awe and flow, and in that space, our purpose unfolds.

You can play the game of life in a much more meaningful way. It will require taking a leap into the unknown, wholeheartedly saying yes to the journey. If you do, I cannot guarantee "success" in the way you may view success right now, but I can assure you, there will be so much joy in the journey regardless of the destination. I trust as you hear and read the words, what needs to resonate with you will. One sentence might be all you need to live a life in flow and when we connect to our individual purposes, we will connect with others to solve puzzles and problems which evolve humanity.

Do you wonder what this life, your life, is all about? What are YOU here to contribute that will add value? How do you intentionally create a life full of meaning, doing something that brings you joy, while assisting your soul to evolve? If you are reading this, perhaps like me, you have found yourself at a crossroads of what was, and what is yet to become. Our school systems need a serious upgrade, and until that happens, we are left to figure out who and how we want to show up in the world.

Kindling your flow is an individual journey of discovery. From the moment you are born, there are aspects of what makes you, you. Intentionally and thoughtfully tapping into some attributes from the flow life funnel as outlined on the following pages, can provide you with a road map to a fulfilling career or hobby. These tools can assist in ah-ha moments that will help you create a life with positive motion toward joy and experiences with deeper meaning and purpose.

Doing something you love everyday creates more harmony in your life. Figuring out what that something is, can be a challenge. Life is hard. Being a human is not all rainbows and roses. Acceptance of the full range of human emotions is one step to getting to the starting line of creating a life in flow. To give yourself the best shot at creating more joy, first and foremost is to work through your "crazy town" blocks. Get rid of the rocks you are holding onto. Forgive yourself and others for past (and future) transgressions. Hold as much peace and love as you can for your journey and toward those in your awareness. When we let go of what weighs us down, we are free to flow wholeheartedly. There will always be work for us to do within ourselves. Self-evolution is an infinite process of existing.

One day I sat down in front of a giant white board and started to draw out the layers to what would become the FLOW Life Funnel. I thought about what choices I had made when I started a nonprofit in college. I thought about all the brilliant people I had heard on podcasts who seemed, like me, to find a flow with their careers. What did we all have in common? Could I figure out the puzzle pieces so that we can intentionally create a life in flow, beyond the occasional flow states?

How do we move with more ease through and with the life we are experiencing?

When we can be conscious and fully aware of our own self-leadership, we make room for figuring out our FLOW Life Funnel. Be open to what is inside of you and right around you. There is so much potential and desire within you that wants to come out and create beauty in this world. You can have peace with what was, be hopeful for what can be, and be present to the current moment so you can Follow Life's Opportunities Wholeheartedly (FLOW).

Happiness comes when one is in pursuit of something that kindles the deepest desires of the heart. Joy in life comes from embracing the creation process as much as the sweet moment of final creation. When our days are filled with mundane and mindless tasks, the heart energy of life, passion, and love are depleted. The ordinary will dull out the light and make it hard to discover our essence. Knowing ourselves wholeheartedly is never impossible. It is always there; it just may need a little attention.

Refueling passion comes from filling the heart with progress toward a worthy endeavor. Pursue something that can cultivate devotion. To FLOW, spend each day laying a brick toward something your heart finds valuable. Listen to your intuition and be courageous.

Some will choose to push against their natural FLOW, and that is okay, too. Those that push against their own FLOW are still working through attachments, expectations, and traumas. This is part of the current human condition. We learn and grow through the small and large traumas of life. They help mold us. They teach us what it means to be human, what it means to feel pain and suffering and they provide us opportunities to learn and offer forgiveness. I believe there is a new way of showing up that will offer a higher quality of life.

Jay Shetty, a college student with aspirations of pursuing a corporate life, met a monk and it changed his life. Although he had never met a monk before, he was open to the experience, willing to let the opportunities into his life he followed how he felt. After schooling, he left the corporate path to become a man without worldly needs. After several years living the life of service, he was counseled to leave the monastery so that he could make a bigger impact in the world. Today, Jay Shetty has become a major positive force in the social media space. He Followed Life's Opportunities Wholeheartedly and today is living a beautiful life in flow, still aligned with his mission and purpose to be of service to humanity.

You don't know what you don't know; so living open to information and experiences is powerful. Exploring your world will allow you to fill your FLOW funnel with many options and let something amazing shake out. No experience is a waste of your time or energy. Each moment of your life builds upon the others. What can you learn and use from your past experiences?

You can pour yourself into the top of the FLOW Life Funnel and come out with options for what path you want to go down. It will give you clarity on your life purpose. The FLOW Life Funnel will assist you in discovering new combinations of what is possible for your life, help you to think outside the box, and push you into courageous moments, which will enhance your human experience. When pursuing that which comes out the bottom, you might feel inadequate, want to self sabotage, give-up, or think, "Who am I to hold this new identity?" You are powerful, unique, talented, and a very important piece to the larger puzzle that is this life and our collective evolution. When you step into your flow, you allow space for others to do the same, and together, we will create more effective, loving and supportive systems.

I believe the closer science and spirituality get, the closer we will be to knowing more truths about who we really are and how to live to our fullest potential, most or even all of the time. I believe we are closer to nature than we understand. We are a system of algorithms, both individually and collectively. We can either live in FLOW and its varying degrees of clarity, or paddle upstream. They are both valid human experiences that offer data back to the source, in addition to creating power downstream or learning upstream. You may also choose to sit out completely and watch the water go by for a bit. Rest and rejuvenation play an important part of the human cycle, especially when one has been paddling upstream for so long and has gotten washed down and then washed up on shore. For those tired of the movement, the thought of getting back into the river of life is terrifying. Nothing is wrong with taking a hard pause on life. Starting again in a new phase or chapter can be scary. We fear the unknown, but we are also designed to walk through it.

Courage is where life wakes up and will always be rewarded. Everything tips into the positive once courage is executed. According to Dr. David R. Hawkins in Power vs. Force, "The critical response point in the scale of consciousness calibrates...with Courage. All attributes, thoughts, feelings, associations, entities, or historical figures that calibrate higher make subjects strong. This is the balance point between weak and strong attractors, between negative and positive influence, and between truth and falsehood."

It takes the most courage to work through your "stuff." It takes great courage to own "your stuff" and then, darn it life; you ask us to muster up more courage to step into a dream...YES! When the dream is flowing, you can put your arms back, take a deep breath and truly enjoy the ride. However, it then takes courage to be willing to adapt and flow with the dream freely, or to "what is next?" because that need is no longer there. Are you ready to do what is needed next; let us get to serving in a new, expanded, potentially different way? It takes courage to put others' needs before your own. The ideal is a balance of self care and using your essence to be courageous for those who cannot do it for themselves...yet.

So when you are ready to step into the FLOW Life Funnel with a full desire to really know, that is when it will produce the most efficient and successful outputs. All attachments to outcomes should be checked at the door. All expectations of what it needs to look like and/or who needs to be involved should also be left behind. It is about the journey, the discovery of what is possible when you truly look around, look within, let go, and let creation unfold.

When filling in your FLOW Life Funnel, consider asking those around you what they think your interests, passions, talents, and strengths are. Sometimes, we can't see what we possess. Asking those around you, even those you don't know well, to let you know what attributes they see in you is helpful when completing your own funnel. They may suggest attributes you never thought you exhibit, but you do! And knowing how others perceive you is valuable information.

When you can filter through the FLOW life principles, and hold space for wherever you are in life today, right now, you are left with the most refined essence of yourself. From this place, take small steps toward what it is you want to create, feel, be, or do. You are the gold miner of your life. The stream you are sifting for gold in is everything that makes up you. As you sift through the eight layers with self-honesty and openness, only the most pure of intent is left. That is the gold! That essence can be used as a guiding tool to lay a path that will add deep devotion to your FLOW journey at this time.

The eight key elements to get curious about, gain wisdom around, and seek personal clarity on, are as follows: Intuition, Interests, Strengths, Talents, Passion, Belief, Need, and Pool of Creativity. I have researched various successful people's lives, and each of these elements has played an intricate part in their success. When the conscious awareness focuses on SELF (you, Seeking Evolution to Live Fully) and these eight principles, willing to let creativity flow through the funnel freely, flow is born. The deeper we love, while maintaining a healthy relationship with the more challenging parts of being a human, the more magically our life will unfold. What if you had a flashlight that could light your journey as you create additional flow in your life?

I am going to briefly tap into the eight principles of the FLOW Life Funnel so you can start to explore them for yourself. Use a blank piece of paper. You will find questions throughout the sections you can journal about, talk about, and ponder. At the end of each section, there are activities to assist you with your journey. Feel free to reach out to me (www.set2love.com or www.evapayne.com) if you have questions, are looking for additional guidance in exploring your funnel, or with what steps you could take next.

When you can pull together the eight different components in a collaborative way, the funnel is working. We are each unique and individualized, so I try to make no assumptions about what will work for you. I suspect for some this will be "the answer they were waiting for", while for others it may feel like "a waste of time." However you perceive, interpret, transform the information in these words is for you to implement or not. Trust YOUR OWN intuition. Take what works, and leave the rest. In the end, I would love for you to believe that you are here to fill a need using

12

your essence. I know you are here to make a difference, even if that difference affects no other soul but your own. It begins with you, and how you feel, live, or interpret the world around you. See the good and your ability to add to it - that is how we evolve together toward the betterment of us all. Thank you in advance for your time!

THE EIGHT PRINCIPLES OF THE

FLOW LIFE FUNNEL

Principle One

INTUITION

So, what is intuition? Ask yourself what you have heard about intuition. What do you believe it to be, if anything? Where have you heard people talking about it? What sounds like intuition to one person might be something different to someone else. One person might say it's "knowing". Another might attest it's "the still small voice inside your head." Another might say it's God. Another will have a scientific explanation behind intuition. To me, it doesn't matter what you believe or where it comes from. As long as you recognize you have some level of intuition that is all we need to start.

If intuition is foreign to you, please take the time to research the heck out of it and trust what feels right. What makes the hairs on your arm stand up? What is the subtle nagging voice that says, "Do this or do that..." until you finally listen and amazing results come to pass? What action does it take to listen to courage, follow through with tangible steps, and create where nothing existed before?

Many of the greatest innovators, leaders, mentors, students, and creators, all attribute success to intuition. Intuition is taking a chance on what is possible, what could one day be. Listening to your intuition takes being brave and stepping into the river. You are on the raft of intuition, trusting yourself fully. Allow the journey to unfold with intuition as a best friend along for the ride. Einstein said, "The intuitive mind is a sacred gift and the rational mind is a faithful servant. We have created a society that honors the servant and has forgotten the gift." It is science and spirituality coming together that will produce the greatest advancements in human evolution...Einstein knew it to be true. Can you live open to the possibility?

I have dozens of stories, and I will share a few in this section, where a thought came into my mind to take action and when I acted on the nudge, I was blown away with the outcome. Intuition is not emotional. Think of it as a suggestion from the universe that can be captured when our mind is clear from the clutter of rumination. In this open space, we can form a connection with something magical.

When I hear that still small voice say for example, "Tell her she is pretty," or "Compliment her," I just do it. I don't even think twice. What really boggles me is how people respond. Generally speaking, others have a difficult time taking in the compliment. They will deny it, question it, make excuses for it, or try to play it down. I have heard comments such as, "Oh this...it was on sale," or "You think so?" instead of, "Thank you." I used to brush off the compliments as they would come in, but now that I pass them out as they come into thought, I try my best to also receive them when they come in from another.

I have seen where simple compliments can bring another to tears. I have also experienced when listening to intuition and performing a kind act can have a profound impact. Once while grocery shopping, I heard the little voice suggest I should give my scarf (which I had just purchased) to a sweet Mom who passed by and offered me a compliment on it. I said the practiced, "Thank you" and as I pushed my cart past her and her daughter, the little chime went off and the notion to give her my scarf popped in. "Nooooooo!" I begrudgingly thought. "I love this scarf." But, I turned my cart around and offered her the scarf. She, of course, didn't want to accept it at first, but I told her I knew where to get a new one, and it was my pleasure to give it to her. We went our separate ways and a few aisles later, her daughter approached me and said, "You have no idea what that moment meant to my Mom. I told her she should tell you." I walked with her back to where her Mother was waiting. She proceeded to explain to me how my act of kindness was the nicest gesture anyone had done for her in a long time and she needed some goodness in her life. She had just returned from visiting her husband in the hospital who was really struggling with cancer and whose prognosis wasn't looking good; she cried and we embraced.

I was stunned at what transpired upon listening and acting on that little voice. Call it chance, right place, right time, synchronicity, or divine intervention … I am grateful the experience happened regardless of how it came to be. Through various small and large experiences, I have learned to trust my intuition. I am also getting better at listening. Intuition gets stronger and stronger the more you exercise it. Although I don't have the data to back that statement up, my experience definitely tells me this. I'll bet you will find that it works this way for you, too.

While on a walk a few weeks ago, I was listening to a song that reminded me of my Mom. I had not heard the song in a few years. Intuition said, "Send it to your Mom." So, without hesitation, I screenshot it and sent it over. The next day, she replied, "Weird. What made you send that?" I called her right away because I knew this was one of those "follow your intuition and see what happens" moments. She proceeded to tell me that right prior to me sending the screenshot of the song, my sister told my Mom that she could not get this same song "Calling All Angels" out of her head - a song she had not thought about in years. It reminded her of when she was younger. My Mom, Step-Dad, brother, and sister, Paige, would go to a nearby city and shop on Saturdays. She was recalling those being memories she cherished and then, BAM, I sent my Mom the text with that exact song screenshot on my phone from my walk. My sister thought maybe I was psychic. I believe this moment happened so we could see the example intuition can play in our lives.

When it comes to what you could be doing to pursue your deepest heart's desires, if you listen, you will feel pulled to act. Be open to what is possible. Spend time researching your best outcome. Talk to people who are doing what you want to be doing - or think you want to be doing. Follow up on every hunch even if it leads to nothing. Go on a walk and be open to ideas, then move toward them. Do not let fear hold you back from sending that email, applying for that job, starting the hobby, taking that class, or talking with that person when it keeps coming up in your mind. There is a force outside of us, offering "advice or guidance" and what can it hurt to courage up and take the leap? You will never know what is possible if you do not ask, do not try, or do not lay bricks toward your current desired path.

Intuition connects us to energy outside ourselves. It does not come from the ego. Intuition is there to help, lead, guide, and offer suggestions. When we can form a relationship with our own intuition, trust it, show gratitude for it by listening to its prompts, we will be blessed beyond measure with experiences we never dreamed would be possible. How will you build and follow your intuition?

Raise Your Intuition Activities

Activity 1: Don't keep the good inside, share it!

Over the next week, when you think a positive thought about someone else, share it with them! Perhaps you are checking out at the market, or in class, online in social media, in a group of strangers watching a game, or even simply in a conversation with a friend; share the good words coming into the forefront of your mind. If it is resonating in your heart, it is there for a reason. You are a messenger, not a storage unit, of positive comments. Honor the message; thank your intuition for bringing it out of your subconscious and placing it on your heart, by speaking the positive thought.

Activity 2: Listen to the "I should ..."

When the small voice or hunch comes in and asks you to follow up, or go and do – then do it. Perhaps it's double-checking you turned off the stove, or to call a friend and check in, or to send an email, etc. Listen to the, "I should ..." because it is your intuition telling you to go and do something.

Activity 3: Be Present in Your Interactions with Others

When you are engaging in conversations with others, practice listening skills. First seek to understand. Put yourself in their shoes, ask questions and refrain from giving advice until you are really clear on all sides of "the story." Do not try to "one-up" the other(s) with your own story. Put your phone away and be fully present with 100 percent of your attention. Set boundaries if needed (timeframes, subjects you are not ready to discuss, etc) and speak your truth if/when needed.

Activity 4: Keep track of the synchronicities

Write or take pics of the moments or signs of synchronicity in your life. These "coincidences" have more meaning than meets the eye. Remember them!! Text yourself, take a picture, or journal about the synchronicities that happen in your day. You will start to see a pattern. What are the themes? What do you think it means? If you are unsure, ask for help in understanding these moments.

Activity 5: See a Need and Fill It

There will be moments in your day when you see a need. Be the one to fill that need as often as possible. There are needs looking to be met everyday and they are designed for your growth! You are the person to meet them! Put any feelings of "awkwardness" aside and step into the discomfort of the need to fill it. You will gain a deep sense of human connection, purpose, synchronicity, and perhaps a new lifelong friend.

Activity 6: Roll the Dice

Practice guessing what two numbers will come up on a pair of dice you are rolling. Clear your mind, see yourself rolling the dice, what numbers do you see? Roll the dice until those two come up! The more you practice, the less times you will take to roll the dice for those two to show up! Setting an intention, even in something as simple as rolling dice to an outcome you desire, will prove to you that there is power in intentions.

Principle Two

INTERESTS

The second principle in the FLOW Life Funnel are interests. What captures your attention and time? What are you drawn toward wanting to know more about? What are you curious about? What do you find yourself looking up online or talking about in conversations? What could you talk about for an hour straight? What do you enjoy doing, seeing, exploring, studying, or participating in? These are your collection of interests. Write them down ... all of them!

It is important to know where the themes are in your personal circle of interests. You may have 100 things that interest you, or you may be unsure if you even have one. Either way, this is a journey of self-discovering. Go back to when you were a child, what did you like to do? How did you joyfully spend your time? Knowing what interests you, and continuing to add to this list, will keep you in moving forward toward FLOW. If you can prioritize your list of interests, even better! Do you see a theme in the things that interest you?

Form a list of all your interests and continue to add to it as you move through your days. Actively seek out new information. Once you do, you will see new interests emerging and maybe others dropping off. Be open to changing up your current list of interests. Ask yourself if your interests can further humanity into an energy of LOVE. Do your interests bring others down? Perhaps you are interested in an activity or experience, but to enjoy it, you must negatively impact another's life. You may choose to still partake, however, please consider what you are creating. My dream is to continue to see creations in FLOW by LOVE, and this effort to move consciously toward oneness.

Stretch for new interests. Actively seek after interests you didn't know you had until you tried them. I would venture to say that you, or someone you know, tried something one day and got sucked into the culture of a new way of being. They would have had no clue they even liked until they tried it!

This is where values come in. If you value new experiences over safety, you will choose the new experience regardless of the consequences. This is true unless you value the safety of not dealing with the consequences over dealing with the potential risks.

Choices come down to values. Every choice you make is always based on what you value more in life. Look at a choice someone makes and really peel the back of the layers to find the real intent, the heart of the matter which is the core or the value. We make choices, thousands of them, each and every day. We choose when to wake up, what to eat, how to dress, act, be, do ... all of it; it is a choice. It is how we choose to show up right now. Are we interested in being a person who engages in_____, or believes _____, or hopes for _____ , or tells _____ . Our choices, especially with the internet, are monitored, surveyed, and sold. We are all being influenced by what is around us. This is human nature. My estimations are since the dawn of mankind, we have demonstrated the ability to influence others, for better or worse. The technology has simply caught up to influence us, and we are just now waking up to this new form of persuasion.

You may think you like basketball because in your entire life you were exposed to basketball. Your parents loved basketball so they enrolled you, you played and you were good. Your Mom and Dad were decent players, and you received some natural athleticism through "basketball player genes." You go on to play in college and get recruited to the NBA. You play for a few years and retire due to injury. You were good at it; you were willing to put in the work. You were willing to deal with the bag of rocks you had to carry to make it a priority; you valued "it" (the success, the game, the fame, the wins and losses, the comradery, etc) more than whatever else you could have been spending your time doing - And that is how values work.

But now, you are injured. While going through physical therapy, you are trying to figure out what now. What do I do now? My life was basketball; all my interests are in basketball. I only know basketball. Could I love anything else even close to as much as I loved basketball? The answer is YES! I know that the answer is yes. It doesn't make sense on a scientific or spiritual level for the answer to be no at 29 ... or 45 ... or 85. The answer is always, yes. Perhaps you are twenty-nine, and never did anything you really liked and you reside on the other end of the spectrum for the basketball player, or perhaps you're the basketball player and only played to please your parents, but never really loved playing in the first place?

Our deeply rooted interests have probably always been present in our lives. For me, I have always loved putting on shows. When I was a kid, my siblings and I would write scripts, which included full blown choreographed lip sync routines, acted out jokes, and sometimes horrible magic. We would have an emcee, set up our living room as a theatre, and host these evening performances for our parents and their friends. In high school, I was the commission of communication reading the morning announcements to the school each day over the school intercom system. In college I was a theatre and broadcasting major and began working at a radio station at 19. Four years into my time with KFRX in Lincoln, NE I was on the morning show. I have used my communication and "performing" skills throughout my life. Today, I host a podcast with my best friend and am the President of my local Toastmasters Club (a worldwide community based public speaking organization). I have always had an interest in becoming an effective communicator and through each of my experiences, I have cultivated my talents and skills in this area. Oh, and we do have a lip sync night at our summer camps and you can bet the staff do a full-our choreographed routine right along with the cabins - when at camp! What interests have you had since you were young and how have they touched your life along its journey? What new interests are peaking up asking you to pay attention a little more?

Exploring interests throughout your life is essential to finding FLOW. When we see the multitude of areas of interest we have in life, we grow to a larger, more open version of oneself. Continue to hone in on what REALLY interests you, even if you do not know where it will take you. Seek information and expand your interests so that life can open up to possibilities. You don't know what you don't know and it is time to find out!

Discover Your Interests

Activity 1: Write down 10 interests you had in grade school, 10 in high school, 10 in college/20's. Is there a theme?

Activity 2: Create a top 10 interest list. Add one new interest to your list once a week until you have a list of 50 areas of interest. Add possible interests to explore.

Activity 3: Ask the people who know you best to share with you what they think your interests are. What do you talk about, bring up, find yourself engaging in when you are with them?

Principle Three: STRENGTHS (fixed) & Principle Four: TALENTS/SKILLS (growth):

Y ou CANNOT be anything you want to be. I know that is not a quote you would see from an optimist. However, it is simply true, and being an optimist doesn't mean living with your head in the clouds. It is vital that you are self aware to live by FLOW. Part of obtaining a clearer picture of who you are, who you can be, and a vision or path toward that outcome, is knowing your strengths and talents - and to me, they are different and equally important.

I love music! I listen to instrumental music when I write. Music can move me to tears or motivate me to push harder. I appreciate the strengths and talents of those who see music in all its beauty. I honor those who can play or sing with almost effortlessness. I am amazed how music can create or support a movement. Music changes lives and I wish I could write, or play, or sing, or contribute to the world of beautiful sound, but no matter how much energy I put into becoming a decent musician, it will never happen. It will never happen because since childhood, my brain has a difficult time understanding the concepts of music notes. When I look at sheet music, I see notes that go up and down, but that is it. I might as well be reading another language, because that is what it is to me. Knowing where I am strong, and where I am weak creates expanded self-awareness.

I have always had a difficult time with learning other languages, and music is no exception. In addition, I cannot ever remember lyrics and the idea of different instruments playing together, to create a masterpiece, sends me to awe. I know that while I LOVE music, I do not have any innate strengths in this area and I have not invested ample time into developing talents or skills in this area, primarily because the language is not one that comes in with ease or flow. Knowing what your innate strengths are then deliberately enhancing them, and investing in talents/skills that drive creativity, passion, awe, wonder, or curiosity, is key to obtaining a FLOW life.

Our strengths last a lifetime. Our talents and skills grow and evolve over a lifetime. Our interests change over a lifetime, and our passions are what keep us fueled for a lifetime. It is well worth your time to become clear on what your talents and strengths are, as early as possible in life, and then nurture them! It is also important to help others around you build these aspects of self-awareness and self care.

Strengths, to me, are the attributes we are born with. These are those traits we have exemplified since we were a child. They are an innate part of who we are, at our core. For example, I have always been a positive person, trying to see all sides to an experience. I have also been able to think strategically and out-of-the-box ... always. I can also step into a leadership role with ease and comfort when needed. These are strengths that came with this body. You have your own set of strengths and if you are not aware of what they are, you can find out. Online assessments such as "StrengthsFinder 2.0" and "StandOut" helped me to see what I already intuitively knew. Receiving a validation, through an assessment, made it more clear for me. I can also look back at my childhood self and think, "What was Eva at eight-years-old really good at?" and answers come in that way, too.

If you have children or siblings, and you take a moment to really think about what makes them consistently stand out of the crowd throughout their lives, you will see their strengths. When you can be objective and honest about what has always made you special, you will see your own strengths. From this place of open awareness, your strength and energy can be moved in a direction that is intentional, full of love, and brings joy to you through filling needs around you. That is living by FLOW.

Talent and skills, to me, are the manifestation of interests and passion. To the extent one focuses on putting heart, mind, and body energy into one's interest and passion; this will dictate the level of success in said talent development. A person in FLOW will have high levels of both interest and passion awareness, and manifesting in motion through everyday life.

Talent is the acquired skills one gains through various human experiences. It has been suggested that the more time spent in nurturing a talent, the higher the level of success one will bring to pass. Being self-aware of your interests is key to understanding where you could have a talent that can be nurtured. For example, if you love dogs, you own dogs, you like dog pics and videos on social media, you volunteer at an animal shelter, you talk to your pets and others as if they are children, then you have a STRONG interest in dogs. It is therefore reasonable to suggest you would be in FLOW if you explored how you spend your time, talents, and treasures in nurturing a talent that has to do with dogs. That is a strength - to love and appreciate life in all forms, as equal to all other life - and a talent in dog training, dog grooming, veterinary, pet psychology, the health benefits to owning pets, etc is well within your wheel well. And nurturing this interest in dogs, this clear passion through action, will help lead you to FLOW.

Nothing is ever wasted. I have a long list of talents that I hardly touch intentionally, anymore. Yet,

I am amazed when they come back around to serve me in a new way. For example, I studied theater in college. I spent four years learning how to create and present a story on stage, and yet I never stepped foot on a stage in any real way post college. Was this a waste of a degree, time, and money? Was this a waste of a talent? Perhaps to some, yes. To me, I can see how the assets I gained in college helped me in my adult life, both personally and professionally. I learned vulnerability. I was surrounded by creative, loving people. I learned to present in front of a crowd. I learned empathy, through character analysis and development. I learned how to stop, breathe, and listen. I learned that an idea can manifest into a production (seeing it happen). I learned how to produce an event from nothing but an idea (doing it myself). Studying theatre is the foundation to who I am as a professional adult, even though it does not manifest itself in the traditional ways many might suspect with this degree.

The talents I nurtured in college still served me through the development and implementation of starting and running a nonprofit. And the talents and strengths I nurtured while running a nonprofit summer camp for youth impacted by HIV/AIDS, and those who require behavioral intervention, has led me to this point in my life. No talent or strength is wasted when you are in alignment with FLOW.

I chose to start a nonprofit while in college, as a theatre major, while working on a morning show at the #1 radio station in Lincoln, Nebraska when I knew nothing about how to do this because what I did know was this:

1) I loved and knew summer camps. I had gone almost every year, from grade school through college.

2) I believed in the power and magic of summer camp.

3) I had enough knowledge in the area and could envision the end before I began... even though I was very flexible with what it looked like, just dreaming about it made my heart pump loudly.

4) I had past experience of starting things I had no idea how to start and was successful.

I put together a holiday drive in high school for kids in need. I helped lead a high school cheer team that became leaps and bounds, more notable than years prior. I was VP of membership at my sorority. I produced "The Yellow Boat," a children's play without help from another adult. I knew I could create "stuff," so why not this?

This venture, Camp Kindle, would be the test of what happens when I take my interests, talents, strengths, and passions to listen to the intuition that said, "Eva, there is a need that you can fill if you only believe and step courageously into the familiar unknown. Together, we will create something almost magical."

When we are in flow with our project, we lose the sense of time, our focus is heightened, our energy is moving in a forward motion that produces synchronicities and awe moments. When we are creating from a flow space, we feel as though we have magic powers. When our interests, strengths, and talents line up to fully engage the endeavor we are putting our energy into, we move with more ease, clarity, determination, focus, and ambition to see it through, no matter what, because the journey captures our heart. The end product, or "destination" is the cherry on the sundae. The more of our essence we put into our careers, projects, hobby's, or experiences, the sooner the effort turns from "work" into passion. And then, we are unstoppable!

Discover the You that is Really You

Activity 1: Write down your top five strengths. If you do not know what your strengths are, search out an online assessment (There are many such as Strength Finder). Do you feel as though you have used these strengths through your experiences? Do you work to improve them?

Activity 2: Write down five to ten talents or skills you have nurtured over your lifetime. How did/do those serve you today? What would you like to get even better at? What new skill or talent would you like to acquire and why?

Activity 3: Do you see a connection in how your strengths and talents have worked side-by-side in your life? Is there an activity you could do this week that would tap into as many of these attributes simultaneously?

Activity 4: Take your list of top five talents and top five strengths, put them on one sheet and place it somewhere you will see everyday. Pick one a day and each time you drink water, hold that attribute in your heart, think of one way it has served you, thank it, and drink your water. Tying the strength or talent to something you already do everyday (such as drinking water), will enhance the overall appreciation and self-awareness of your gifts.

Principle Five

PASSION

Passion can move people. Passion can be used to build people up, and it can be used to take people apart. Passion has created change for the better and for the worse as well. Passion is a driver, a mover, a shaker, a human magnet, and it always wants to win. So, what are you passionate about and why? Let's be passionate about creating a world that sees love in a new supportive way where we do not need to be perfect. We can be passionate about leaving room for growth and the beauty of imperfection, while we each figure out how to be true to where we are today, right now. There is no clear line of good and evil, there is simply one's own beliefs that determines what is "right." The longer we live open, the more we will come to experience that life is lived in the shades of gray.

So, we HAD to be created by SOmeThIng, SoMeWherE, right? It's all too perfect to have been left up to chance. And with that notion, I was open to an array of possibilities. After forty-two years of living, I have seen too many connections, felt too much pain, so much love, and too much shame to not believe that it is all beautiful and divine. See, with each experience, I was able to choose how to respond, and I made the best choice I could have made, given the knowledge I knew at the time. And then, if I failed, the only way for me to grow again was to learn the lesson in my own way.

Therefore, I experienced growth from my pain. And, God willing, I can stay consciously grounded in life, in gratitude, in service, in LOVE, in peace, in positivity. Things will come that will hurt, but that is an opportunity for you to climb up to the next level. So, conquer your current biggest FEAR, and step into SELF LOVE to FLOW. Life is beautiful; choose to see it in every person. Choose to see the beauty in every experience. Choose to see it in every FEAR. But ALWAYS choose to follow your hearts' deepest love. The only way into wholehearted FLOW is through the reframing of love.

Wherever you land in life, into whatever faith or belief system, make sure to Live Open and Value

Everything. When and if you feel confusion, stress, or anxiety around a particular belief system (and this is ANY belief you are holding onto) because the weight of what is expected is not in flow with your essence, it is okay to say, "No thank you. This is no longer working for me," and walk away...just like an old haircut. The only expectation you need to "live up to" is your own hearts' desires. You will survive and you will thrive, because you activated your hearts' power. We all have a tremendous amount of energy that flows through our hearts. It is a super power inside all human beings. It is also known as passion. We are our own creators of our own personal reality at every moment, in the present moment. Right now. You are choosing to be here. Why?

Now pause. Maybe for a long while and really just think about that question. Why are you here, right now, in this moment? What thoughts do you have? Are there negative parts that need LOVE? Shine your light into those areas, even if it hurts a little. The more you are willing to see, the faster you will grow into knowing and trusting your own flow. It will not matter what anyone says to you. When you have a heart passion driven life MISSION, come hell or high water, you will make it happen! AND, you will also NOT compromise on the outcome you envision most! That drive is what improves the world.

Dream and TAKE ACTION with your whole essence. What does or could make you the happiest when you do it, or experience it? Let yourself dream as if you were five-years old, laying in the soft grass at sunset with a best friend, and she asks you, "If you could experience anything in this human body, what would you want that to be?" AND THEN, let your imagination go wild, while leaving room for the what if's and the possibility that living in flow is real. Be open to where you have been and where you can go. Let go of all your current identities for a few moments to allow for creativity to move through your imagination. You may be surprised what ideas come in when you are free from the beliefs and labels you are holding onto. I am not suggesting you should drop them, just be open for a few minutes to adapting or evolving your current belief systems, especially if it says someone else is wrong, it drives fear inside you, or restricts your desire to be creative. Love is open and can see the good in even the darkest of spaces.

Interests kindle passions. If you do not know what you are passionate about, you have not spent enough time finding out what interests you in the world. Open up and start doing or learning something new, big or little, just start. Something, one day, will grab you at your core. These ideas can come from exploring the world you have access to right now. You can find awe in watching a documentary, educational videos online, or inspiration from walking through a bookstore or library with an intention to kindle a new interest, which can lead to a passion.

You might think, "I don't have time for anything new?" I would ask you, how important is discovering your FLOW? We make time for the things that matter. Your FLOW should be at the top of your list. Just walking around with an open mind and heart will allow for new interests to plant alongside your road to FLOW. You will start to notice "it" popping up around you. That is your subconscious asking you to take a better look. There is a connection and within exploring that connection, you will discover your passions. There are many inside you, so don't be afraid of breaking your patterns and exploring your own curiosity.

Passion is that feeling of falling in love. It is what gets you out of bed in the morning with enthusiasm. It is not fixed, but rather fluid. Passion moves in intensity, but has life always pumping. Passion is the life force that brings courage and bravery to the forefront. Passion is falling in love with the movement, the idea, the vision, the possibilities, the hope and belief of what is possible if only ... AND THEN, doing it! That is where the rush of passion exists.

Passion will ground you and passion can bring about your wildest dreams to visualization. For those who have a high feminine energy and very little masculine, or reversed, finding a passion in alignment with one's interest, talent, and strength can be the motivating factor to tip you into a more balanced life. There are challenges in the pursuit of passion. Passions are discovered along the human experience; so the more you discover about life, the more likely you are to discover a passion.

If your passion will solve a problem in humanity, bring about peace, LOVE, and positivity, then you NEED TO BE DOING IT!! For goodness sakes - get to it. I am counting on you. I am doing my part, to the best of my ability, for you, so please get to your passion because the world needs you to show up as your most positively-evolved self in each moment. Being eager to create using your essence is where passion is fueled. No matter how bumpy the road is, you need to get out there and journey through. Albert Einstein said, "I never made one of my discoveries through the process of rational thinking." Self doubt will hinder the creative process. We thrive in imagination and creativity. Being open to how to solve our challenges on a micro and macro level will prove our ability to succeed. Falling in love with life, wherever you are in the journey leads to more flow. Find what drives you to want to create and be courageous with the actions you take! Be willing to take a path you are unsure of, or goes against what you thought was real or possible. The greatest discoveries come from stepping through the door of openness and into a series of synchronicities.

Cultivate Passion

Activity 1: Think about or journal a time when you were really passionate about something you were doing in life. How did you get there? What made it so special and connected to your heart?

Activity 2: If you could snap your finger and be in flow on a path toward ANYTHING, what would you pick and why?

Activity 3: Watch, listen, or engage in an activity or experience that brings up the feeling of awe and wonder in your soul. What inspires you toward a feeling of awe? Why?

Principle Six

BELIEF

The power of belief can create what seems like miracles right before your eyes. When you truly believe in someone or something, there is a force that is real and can be measured. I do not know how, but others smarter than myself have spoken about such ideas. If you think of a time in your life when you truly believed in something, I would suspect you would say there was magic around that moment, whatever it was. Belief is worth nurturing in your life, because it will transform your ability to be open, grow, and love.

When I started Camp Kindle, I was so terrified to tell anyone my idea for fear of them laughing at me, or simply expressing the same doubt back at me, that I had in myself. I am not really sure why it was so hard to share the idea, but it was. I had a friend in high school who always professed these large accomplishments that were "just about to happen," but none of them ever did, not one. And I didn't want to be that person - the one with all the talk and no action. I would not declare action until I had enough belief in myself. I also desired at least one other person in my corner who could believe in me, perhaps in even a greater way, and in my potential for FLOW.

I called my former Step-Father, a level headed, grounded, logical businessman and asked him if he thought I, a head-in-the-clouds creative, could actually start a summer camp. He didn't hesitate to respond, "Yes, of course you can do it, but you have a lot to learn." And I did, and I still am. But his straight forward, bold, to-the-point belief was all the fuel I needed to shoot me through the FLOW funnel, and into starting Camp Kindle.

The success cycle kicks in when you start. Once you take the chance and see a win, even the tiniest, babiest win ... it is a step and that IS A SUCCESS. So, if you only improve by .000000001% that is a freaking success and you can do it again. Feel the excitement - you earned it! You will build belief when you combine what you are naturally good at, with what you have learned to be good at (or are learning), in combination

51

with experience and courage. Belief can come from outside of you until you have it within to carry you the rest of the way. Once FLOW kicks in, and the synchronicities start popping up, belief grows exponentially.

The beliefs we hold about ourselves, others, the way the universe works, and what is possible are guiding principles we hold through life that add meaning, purpose and direction. These beliefs are the lense we see and perceive the world through. They help us interpret what is happening around us. Having a strong belief system, or someone who believes in you, is empowering. Our beliefs are birthed and molded through our environments and experiences. They are malleable. Our beliefs around anything can change, they are not static, and they are a moving force in our lives. What you believe is always a choice. You get to believe whatever you want about anything you want. Our beliefs will become our reality, so choose yours wisely.

I interviewed an Olympic figure skating coach. She worked closely with a young skater who was destined to earn gold, and took home silver. When she got on the ice, she was mesmerizing in her ability to interpret the music and move in her routines/programs with flow and awe. She held some strong beliefs, which ultimately did not serve her. If she fell three times on the ice at a rink, she would not skate there again because it was bad luck. While practicing at the Olympics, she had temper tantrums on the ice when her elements and sequences would not go her way. It took a phone call from a Russian energy healer to change her belief about her ability to succeed. The pressure of skating in the Olympics, with the expectation of winning gold, was too much for her to handle. She fell on her program and instead of gold, took silver. This might seem like a win for any of us, but when you compete at that level, for your whole life, for the one shot, and miss it, disappointment is an understatement.

On the flip side, this same coach watched a young man turn pro on the ice and never had the same belief blocks this other young skater had. The coach pondered how one young person struggled with self-belief while the other had none. She came to find out that since this boy was a child, every time he stepped on the ice he said, "I am the King of the ice!" until he was. His self-belief by this simple statement over and over and over again, solidified his own self belief and that led him to great victories without the tantrums and self-doubt.

Even when you do not believe in who you want to become, say it anyway. Embody that belief that you are in line, and your turn will come. You have the tools, support, and ability to achieve your life purpose. You came here with the essence to do and be your deepest heart's desire. Once you have a clear vision of where you want to go, hold it close, use positive words around expressing these desires, see your dream and do not let anyone else's negative beliefs impact your dream. Fear, doubt, and insecurity are the poison to you believing in what is possible for you. How will you build your belief in what is possible for you?

Build Belief

Activity 1: Recognize who supports you and your dreams. Do you have at least one trusted, sound, supportive person? If not, where do you think you could find one? (Life Coach, Mentor, Teacher, Friend).

Activity 2: Ponder or journal about a time when you did not believe in yourself, but having the support of someone else, assisted you to move toward your goal. Reflect on when you did believe in your own potential. What was that experience like for you?

Activity 3: Do something that REALLY scares you (that is safe), and pushes you mentally, physically, spiritually. Journal about how you felt before and after. When have you had to be courageous in your life? How did you feel after?

Principle Seven

NEED

If you don't have anything that particularly impacts your life in a way that drives passion, that is okay. However, if you also have a burning desire to make a difference in this world, then you can find a need so you can fill it. BUT, do not be hasty. Just open your eyes to what is around you. What has come up, over and over again, in your life? What do you gravitate toward? What are the patterns, and can they matter to you?

Dive in, Live Open to all the possible places your heart pulls you to, and then Value Every experience. There are so many needs all around you, every day. You do not need to go out and start a nonprofit. Begin to be intentionally aware of what is happening around you. Have the desire to serve in whatever way would be the most beneficial. Let go of expectations around what the service could/should look like, as even a compliment to a person who needs to hear kind words is filling an important need. Each time you serve, you create an energy of LOVE, peace, and positivity. Serving another is fuel for the soul.

FLOW really starts revving up when we are able to utilize more and more of the aspects to the FLOW Life Funnel. When we become more clear of our essence and are able to put together what interests us, utilizing our strengths and talents, we kindle ideas. Now, when ideas come in, sit with them and see how you feel. Ponder what you can contribute to grow the idea, and once you start to water the idea with action, experiences to support it will come to fruition. Collaborations around ideas, utilizing your circle of influence will bring in new perspectives. Recognizing others' essence, which link nicely into what you want to create, especially if they have different strengths and talents than yours, will add value and power to creating something new.

If you see a need and you can fill it, then do it. If you cannot fill the need you see, but you know someone who can, then tell them. If it is not your need to fill, then simply sit with it for a few moments. Tell the universe ,"I see this need, and I do not know what to do about it. If it is mine to do something with, please give me the guidance and direction I need to fill it. When it is time, if it is mine, I am open to helping fill the need if you need me." Be in true S.E.L.F - L.O.V.E. And leave it ... it is no longer yours unless it comes back around in some way. That is powerful.

Be proactive...but what if you are not seeing anything coming in? What do you do then? How do you find a need and fill it? That is what you are really here to do. I believe one of the actions that bring us the most joy is when we utilize a high percentage of our FLOW Life Funnel attributes to fill a need. We can use our left brain to actively look for what is the biggest need in the community, home, work, etc (wherever/whatever/ you are trying to improve in your neck of the woods). And, we use our right brain for the intuition to know which way to go, thus, allowing the pool of creativity to enter the FLOW Life Funnel.

One place to start is in silence. Sit quietly, or go for a walk and begin to notice all the connections in your life. Everything is connected, and opportunities are abundant. Ponder how you got here to this moment. What are all the circumstances that brought you to this point? How did you get here today, to this moment, in this body, living THIS life, with the talents and gifts, and opportunities you possess? I promise you, your life is not by chance or a waste, or without purpose or meaning. We create meaning and purpose by the actions we take. You have needs someone else can fill and you have gifts to help fill the needs of others. This cycle of sharing our selves, growing, aiming high together, for the betterment of humanity and the planet as a collective, is a noble pursuit.

Even if life is by absolute chance (I do not believe that in my heart, but I need to live open to that possibility), then isn't life better lived being self actualized and using those superhero abilities in a kind way to make a difference? While pain and struggle are part of life, they do not need to be the dominating emotion. When we fill needs, especially when it is a need we feel connected to on an energetic level (feeling the pull to serve literally in your body, mind, and spirit/heart) our lives will change for the better. There is no better medicine than giving. The outcome is joy.

Serving others builds confidence, self-awareness, and meaning. We are all extremely valuable. We all can be served and we all can serve. Therefore, we can all create lives of joy and abundance.

The SELF is like a teeter totter moving lovingly from one side of SELF to the other. We have the logical, everyday SELF here to learn and live with the least amount of suffering as possible. This is truly an inner growth component that takes place over our lives through various experiences. We also have a higher SELF that is creative and empathetic, that wants to take chances and make the world a better place. We move from Seeking Evolution to Living Fully (learning, resting, growing), to Serving, which Electrifies Loving Fully. When we are not focused on replenishing our SELF (self care is so needed in life, and often), then we can move into our higher SELF. This SELF is here to give and fill needs because this self has superpowers that cannot wait to come forth. Learning to love all the versions of you that exist, is key to SELF LOVE. By loving your own short-comings and imperfections, we grant others permission to do the same.

Life is better lived when one another's needs are met. See needs and fill them, find needs and fill them, and/or allow others to fill needs you have right now by letting someone know how you are doing; speak out, because when you voice a need, out loud with kindness, it has power. Filling a real need is a key component to living a life of FLOW.

When I had the idea for Camp Kindle, I didn't have a clue if there were a dozen other camps or programs in the Midwest for children with HIV, or if there were none. I needed to find out if there was a need for a camp. While I wanted to create this organization, it would not have been successful if there were other programs already filling this need. When I did my research, there were no other organizations directly focused on serving youth in the Midwest who were impacted by HIV and AIDS. There were other camps, dozens over the country, but there were also thousands of children living with HIV, and thousands more who had a parent or sibling with the disease. There were too many children not being served. None of these organizations focused on the states that were in my direct circle of influence. Therefore, I saw a need and filled it.

In the end, filling the needs of our world is the most important work you can do right now. You are filled with abilities to heal others, to create products, programs, and movements that will foster improved quality of life for others. Your success is our success. Do not be afraid to stand on the very edge of your comfort level to make someone else's life better. You will be amazed at what you are able to accomplish when you wholeheartedly fill a need you never thought you could do.

Needs are Meant to be Filled

Activity 1: Ponder/Write about the last need you filled. How did it feel? Did you enjoy doing it? When was the last time you filled a need and by doing so, it filled you up with more love and appreciation for life?

Activity 2: What needs your attention? Where do you feel pulled to serve or make a difference? Write a list of at least five ways you can fill needs using your essence.

Activity 3: If you could use your essence to fill a need, and money or time were not an obstacle, what need(s) would you fill? What steps can you take in the next few weeks to create opportunities to connect with this need in a real way?

Activity 4: Do you have an idea, career, or passion you want to pursue? Spend a few hours this week researching who is already doing this work, how are they doing it, and is what you want to do the same or different? What unique aspect would you bring to filling this need?

Principle Eight

POOL OF CREATIVITY

IBM's 2010 Global CEO Study stated, "The effects of rising complexity calls for CEOs and their teams to lead with bold creativity, connect with customers in imaginative ways, and design their operations for speed and flexibility to position their organizations for twenty-first century success."

Creativity is the ability to improve, i.e., to add value. It is the act of turning new and imaginative ideas into reality. If you have ideas but don't act on them, you are imaginative but not creative. Rollo May, an American Psychologist, wrote in The Courage to Create, "Creativity is the process of bringing something new into being...creativity requires passion and commitment. Out of the creative act is born symbols and myths. It's bringing awareness to what was previously hidden and points to new life. The experience is one of heightened consciousness-ecstasy."

A few months back, I listened to Elizabeth Gilbert on YouTube. She wrote "Eat, Pray, Love" and "Big Magic" - which I highly recommend reading, listening to, or at least searching for her interviews. "Big Magic" covers the topic of creativity extensively. Ms. Gilbert is a great example of someone in FLOW. In one talk, she spoke about creativity living outside of us, that we work with creativity to produce whatever we bring forth in the world. Therefore, whatever I create is not all me, but rather some of me (I am the vessel with which the action must be taken to manifest into reality) and there is some kind of divine inspiration from something outside me, something bigger than me. The inspiration (creativity) comes in and I can choose to act or not.

This idea of creativity living outside of us resonated with me on a deep level. At twenty-one, I had no idea how I was going to bring forth an idea in my head, that would not leave me alone, to a hundred people at a summer camp, but I was willing to give it a try and see what happened. I had enough confidence to at least lay a brick a day, until one day, the momentum was flowing, seemingly on its own, with me and hundreds of others in the boat moving along the river of a dream-turn reality, that is Camp Kindle. Every dollar donated, every hour of time offered, every hug given, every kind word spoken was, and is, the collaborative creative power of a community called Camp Kindle.

We brought forth the larger concept, and dozens of staff members helped to create and execute the content. We created a culture where creativity was valued and needed. We wanted our staff to bring their passions, strengths, talents, and interests forward. When we left room for this to occur, we had successful camps. When we were micromanaging, there was more resistance and struggle. When we can learn to let go of what is not in our wheel well and recognize it in someone else's, together we can be stronger, more effective, and overall, more fulfilled.

How do we achieve creating successful programs, organizations, and endeavors? Creativity is the key component to reaching success in FLOW. We can have all our essence realized, but without a way to express it, what value does it bring the world? Some believe that whatever they are doing now in life is what they will be doing for the rest of their life. Others believe there is only one direct path to the end goal. I am suggesting we can live open to creativity. There is not only one path to whatever goal you may have. There are infinite roads to get there (or a least more than you can think of right now) and when we can say, "All right universe, I am open to having this look like whatever it needs to look like," we give permission for the creative waters to start running through our FLOW Life Funnels.

In fact, I heard on a podcast that most young people today will have several jobs in the future at one time. They will be creating their own career through a collection of pursuits. All their eggs will not be in one basket, at one company, doing one thing. Just as I type this sentence, the thought of ongoing repetition, year after year, sounds dreadful to me. As creative beings, we want careers, families, friendships, and communities that are leveling up in kindness, productivity, effectiveness, meaning, etc. Flatline movement is still a movement, however, it is not FLOW. When we are in FLOW, there are waves of brilliance in ongoing ah-ha moments. Those are the moments of pure magic.

Creativity is in all of us. We are creative beings. All we need to do is look around. Everything you see was created in the mind of a person first. However, I would suggest that prior to the thought entering the mind, to which you choose to act or not act on, it was always there waiting for a funnel to open up. Once the funnel is full (you know you are ready to make a difference), the pool of creativity can flow down and use what makes you special to produce an outcome that is unique to you.

If you and I were given the same need - improve the quality of life for a young person as an example- what we would create would be different, but equally valuable. I created a nonprofit and a book. You might create solutions to problems we don't even know exist yet. Perhap reinventing our education system, a new and improved way to execute ideas, resources for parents so they can show up for their children in a more wholehearted way, or an event that brings about connection because your essence is in that world, but together, we are collectively solving a problem and filling needs. The more pure our intent to serve really is, the more creative we can be.

Letting go of needing to figure everything out right now allows space for creativity to do its magic. I could not have predicted a majority of the content I helped create. Do you ever feel as though ideas just pop in? So many of the thoughts and ideas that come to me feel as though they are dropped in from nowhere. Several songs were written with this "download."

According to one article on DigitalMusicNews.com, Daniel Sanchez stated Adele wrote "Skyfall" in less than 10 minutes, and Taylor Swift wrote "We are Never Ever Getting Back Together" in 25 minutes saying, "Randomly, this guy walked into the studio who I had never met before – but I heard of him through my ex – and he made some comment about how he'd heard that we were going to get back together. That was not the case! After he left, I explained the story to Max and said, 'We are never ever getting back together' and someone said we should write that. I just grabbed the guitar and it just happened very randomly. ." She followed the opportunity in front of her and creativity poured through her FLOW Life Funnel to create a hit song.

The Beatles' "Yesterday" was written overnight, The Rolling Stones' "I Can't Get No" Satisfaction was written in 40 minutes, REM's "Losing My Religion" in 10 minutes, Beyonce's "Single Ladies (Put a Ring on It)" in 10 minutes, and Queen and David Bowe wrote "Under Pressure" under 10 minutes. Finally, Ray Charles improvised "What'd I Say" and said, "I had sung everything I could think of. So I said to the guys, 'Look, I'm going to start this thing off, I don't know where I'm going, so y'all just follow me.' And I said to the girls, 'Whatever I say, just repeat after me.'" All these songs, and I am sure countless other creations, came forth quickly and with the help of creativity.

I started drawing my ideas. I am not a very talented artist, but the point wasn't to create art in the form of a portrait; the point was to see my idea, in its entirety, without too many words first. The words would come in too fast at times and I could not type fast enough. Drawing helped me capture the thought, like a photograph, that I can refer back to at any point. The pictures, like the acronym for L.O.V.E. I use in this book, came to me quickly. The process of writing is long; however, the words flow ... most of the time.

What can you do to empty your mind of clutter and partner with creativity? Prior to writing, I take a deep breath and put my mind into a place of receiving. I ask for guidance and support, from whatever powers of good that exist, and I start writing. For me, the belief that someone or something is helping me gives me confidence. Whether it is true or not is irrelevant to me because it works. Therefore, it makes logical sense to believe in something bigger than I, which is ultimately helping me help others, and helping others bring me joy; so it is a cycle of success I enjoy spending my time doing.

One final way to be creative with this funnel is to look at it through the lens of what you are already doing now. How many layers of your funnel match up to what you are doing right now? Do you feel happy, challenged, fulfilled, connected to the way you spend your time right now? Is what you are doing/focusing your time on interesting to you? Is there an ease to it? Does it utilize, maximize, and drive your strengths, skills and talents forward in evolution in a way that brings increased joy? Is there a deep connection to a mission or vision that lights you up inside? Are you filling a need you connect with and do you have someone who is believing in you right now? Can you believe in yourself?

This funnel was designed so that I could see what I already knew, but could not explain in a clear way with logical steps. My hope is that this idea assist you to tap more into who you are so that you can connect to this life in a deep and meaningful way everyday.

Allow yourself the permission to recognize you are a creative being. We all are. What we choose to create, the reality all around you right, is created by you. The lens you see your life through will determine your flow. When we live open to creativity and all that is possible in the name of love, we soar. It is within these creative spaces where imagination runs wildly unapologetically free and innovation is realized. Here is where open, loving, trusting collaborations become our greatest superpower. Creativity is a best friend and is asking us to visit more often. She moves like water. Jump in. Perhaps catch a wave. You and I are welcome anytime. She has so many ideas she wants to share.

Swim in the Pool of Creativity

Activity 1: Write a list of ways you have or do enjoy being creative. What have you learned about yourself while in these creative endeavors?

Activity 2: Walk through a craft store and pick up something new to explore. Try something new just because it sounds fun. How did it feel to step into a new space?

Activity 3: Collaborate on someone else's project or hobby. Offering up your essence on someone else's project can get those creative juices flowing.

Activity 4: Go for a walk with a clear and open mind. Studies show that our minds work more creatively when we are walking rather than sitting down.

Activity 5: Surround yourself with people or activities that inspire you. Being around others who are creative, can inspire your own creativity.

Follow what touches your heart the most. That is always first and foremost.

EXAMPLE OF THE FLOW LIFE FUNNEL IN USE

B elow is an example of how I used the FLOW Life Funnel to help my son, Brayden, see one possible path his life may lead, if he so chooses:

Brayden just came outside after I wrote this sentence to tell me that he just watched the first episode of "The Good Doctor" and cried three times. I had an ah-ha moment as his Mom. When Brayden was in early elementary school, he would often have a play-date with the cutest boy on the Autism Spectrum. They would always have a ball together, but sadly, they moved up North.

Last summer, Brayden volunteered at one of our camps. It is for kiddos with any health challenges; most in our community are on the spectrum. Brayden, who is 12, is unlike his older brother who volunteered and did not have patience for more than half a day...and that is perfectly fine, we all have our own needs to fill in this life. Working with kiddos on the spectrum is not where Coleman will end up, but it is where Brayden may venture in some aspect of his life. As his Mother, I see his desire to connect and I clearly see the need in our communities of children living on the spectrum increasing. I did not know nearly as many youth on the spectrum when I was a child - there is an increasing need for resources for this population, and perhaps he will move towards that, and maybe not. I would certainly add that being connected to those on the Autism Spectrum falls into many of Braydens' FLOW Life Funnel:

Intuition/Empathy: He naturally gravitated to the young boy on the Autism Spectrum. The relationship was never forced, only nurtured. And luckily, us parents saw/knew the connection was genuine, mutually beneficial, and we let it grow.

Passion: I can see it growing - like a light with a dimmer switch, slowly moving up. I can see his deep passion for human connection, for theater. Where it goes, is up to him...not me.

Talent: He is SOOOO Good with the 5-12 year olds at camp. He is mature, patient, and kind. He actually taught in our workshops, and was a camp counselor!

Strengths (since he was born, I could see these things): Empathetic, considerate, open-minded, devoted, a leader among his peers, strategic, and wonderment/curiosity for EVERYTHING, to name a few!

Interests: Summer camp (the kid loves it), comedy, connecting with people, theater, video games, boy scouts, soccer, ...

Belief: I know Brayden can, and will, live a full life and my job is to keep supporting him in exploring his own FLOW Life Funnel - I am helping to create early success cycles, which I believe will give him the leg up as he matures into finding his own FLOW. He is seeing his own success and his confidence this year is off the charts.

Pool of Creativity: Brayden created the courses he taught at the camp, and he liked doing it - it was a creative match. Brayden loves theatre, and he is pretty good at helping to create cool productions at his junior high. Brayden loves exploring anime and all things Japan - who knows how that works in, but somehow, it might...this is where I leave the window open.

POURING THE PIECES INTO THE FUNNEL

I Live Open and Value Everything about who Brayden is at his core. I am doing my best to nurture what is already there, and not try to mold him into who I think he needs to be. At the end of the day, I want to be able to say I did my best and really mean it. How he processes my parenting, is on him. I do my best to see the most fitting opportunities for him, as does he. He has young superpowers, but superpowers nonetheless, and the sooner I can help him tap into them, the sooner he clicks into his own FLOW. We are a team in finding the experiences he can have utilizing all his essence, while leaving space for new ones to come in. We are forever creating. Each day is your own creation, so decide how you want to paint it. What will you put or recognize into your funnel so that you can live more in flow?

Creating a life in FLOW is possible for us. Can we live open to what is possible and find value in each moment? Can we face our fears and step courageously into what we want to create, while managing the ever changing tides? FLOW is a way of showing up to our life everyday. We can be in flow with our relationships, our careers, how we feel about ourselves, our health, and our communities. We are designed, like everything else in nature, to move with more ease, to handle the storms when they show up, and grow with each experience. May we all find our flow.

FINAL THOUGHTS

Can we continue to succeed even when the cards c stack against us? Yes. When life feels so darn hard and you can't see the good, Stop...Really Stop. Then, breathe intentionally for peace. Ask for clarity, for flow, for love to help you see the good in even this very particular situation right now in your life. Then, breathe again. Slow and intentionally rest. "Sit by the River" as a friend would say to me. Then breathe, slow, deep, from the heart and into the belly. Hold it and let it go. Let it all just go.

Let go of the attachments that hold you back. Let go of the expectations. Let go of the outcome and BELIEVE/know that you are doing the best you can, right now, in this moment, and that matters. And THAT is of your highest good. That is aiming high and striving to tip into the 51% pain free kind of moment. You are beautiful. You are here with purpose and to fill a need in someone else's life today. You are here to add value to someone else. You add value to my life just for making it this far through my story.

Listen for the answer. Listen to your intuition. Look for your strengths, if only for a few minutes a day. Acknowledge your talents and nurture them. Know what you like and don't like by trying lots of things and living open. Find value in those who do not see life through your lens, and they may find value in you. We are different, with a vast range of talents and abilities to contribute. Thank goodness this is true! This is how we create. Thank goodness we lead such unique lives. This provides us the opportunity to create from such unique places.

We are magical creatures. If there are alien races, I bet they are watching us in absolute astonishment and saying, "LOOK AT WHAT THEY CAN CREATE!! Look at how they love and look at how they hate." I sometimes think, what if EARTH is a giant "Hunger Games," there are others out there creating our reality, watching our reality, helping us to grow, and even cheering us on. I think there must be some kind of force for good, and force for greatness, because the evidence is astounding. And even if there isn't anything beyond you and me, that is enough to create a force for good. And that push to create beauty in our lives is worth pursuing.

Pour your essence into the Flow Life Funnel and be open to what comes out. Try new experiences that grab your attention. Seek others doing what you think you want to be doing and shadow them for a day. You could also be the first at creating something new. Unapologetically follow what brings you the most joy. There are no timelines, deadlines, or expectations on how your flow life will unfold. Our human experience was never designed to not be challenging or difficult. Life is challenging when you believe it shouldn't be. Our challenges strengthen us, wake us up to our humanness, and offer us a range of opportunities to grow.

The FLOW Life Funnel is a tool, a manual, a guide. Without intentional committed action, it is as if you read the instruction pamphlet and put it back down. You are the architect of your life. Without any action toward a more meaningful purpose driven life, you are still creating a life. You get to choose to step onto a path more in alignment with your soul. One of

THE FLOW LIFE FUNNEL

the most courageous moves you can make is to follow your heart. It will get broken or disappointed along the way. You will wonder if you are making a difference at all or if this path is even going to work out. Stay committed to action and you will not fail. You will be proud of your steps, even if they lead to a deadend and you need to pivot. Let me save you the disappointment now, you will need to pivot, adjust, tweak, and caress your way through your flow life. Thank you for being brave enough to take a chance on a dream, an idea, an aspiration, a hope. Thank you for your time, because your time matters. I am honored you would share yours with me. God knows there are 100 other places you could be right now.

Be kind and flexible with yourself as you explore your flow life funnel. We are all caterpillars outgrowing our cocoons and emerging as butterflies. We do this over and over again through our various identities. Each time we transform, we evolve into a new version of us. Thank you for being a part of my journey and for being open to a new tool that can assist you into discovering your life purpose. May you be courageous

84

in the pursuit of what makes your heart ignite with passion. May you live a life in flow.

Kindle Your Flow,
Eva Payne

ABOUT THE AUTHOR

At heart, Eva is a pioneer and teacher. She has spent over 20 years cultivating leadership and self advocacy skills in thousands of participants through the nonprofit she began while in college, Project Kindle (www.projectkindle.org). She was recognized as a Volvo for Life Award Finalist, twice, and a L'Oreal Woman of Worth. She has been featured in Family Circle Magazine, as a DirecTV Hometown Hero, on the Big 10 Networks "Live BIG", and the summer camp she began, Camp Kindle, has been featured in People Magazine, MTV, E!, and Nickelodeon. She is a self proclaimed "Leadership and FLOW Junkie" with a Masters in Leadership and Management. The FLOW Life Funnel is one idea from her upcoming release "Be Magical." Eva co-hosts a weekday morning podcasts "SET 2 LOVE." She enjoys furthering great nonprofits and causes, energizing others through public motivational speaking, and her greatest joy is being a mom to six children age 9 to 20. She loves getting on a call and strategizing one-on-one on how others can create a life that they cannot wait to wake up to because it is lived in flow! She uses her intuitive ideation to help individuals see what has been there all along!

Feel Free to Reach Out:

www.evapayne.com   www.set2love.com

Made in the USA
Monee, IL
24 October 2021